THE FIGHT FOR AMERICA'S FUTURE

DEFENDING THE SECOND AMENDMENT

By Charlie Kirk

Published By
The Conklin Foundation

TABLE OF CONTENTS

Introduction

I am honored to have the opportunity to write my third book, and my second on this topic in just a few years. This book will detail and analyze the importance of the Second Amendment, hunting, and our founding freedoms -- all of which are very important to me.

Every day I deal with college and high school students who are woefully misinformed about hunting and the Second Amendment. In 2012, right after I graduated from high school, I started a national student movement called Turning Point USA. This organization is now active on over 1,200 college and high school campuses across the country. I founded Turning Point USA because I believe in freedom and limited government and wanted to do something to advance those ideas and principles on college campuses.

In a little over 5 years, Turning Point USA has become the most powerful and most impactful student organization in the country focusing on identifying, training, and organizing students around the ideas of freedom, smaller government, and the Constitution. Turning Point USA also informs young people about their hunting heritage and the Second Amendment.

When the Conklin Foundation asked me to write a second book about this topic for them, I immediately accepted their offer with enthusiasm. Hunting is a critical component of our country's history and it is often misunderstood and intentionally misrepresented by the coastal elites. Teachers mislabel hunting as a meaningless, medieval activity that needs to be outlawed and castigated in our society. Even worse, teachers sometimes single out students who happen to come from a hunting family or a family that own guns. Our school system has become increasingly aggressive against hunting and gun ownership. The more time I spend around America's school system, the more I see that there is a clear agenda to erase our past and completely destroy our gun rights and our hunting heritage.

This book is written for people of all ages, but specifically it is targeted at grade school, high school, and college students. Within these pages I attempt to answer the question of why we have the Second Amendment and why it so necessary in today's world. If one can successfully answer the question of "why" they will be immensely better equipped to debate and win over those who want to abolish hunting and confiscate all the guns in our society.

Finally, towards the end of the book I detail the tactics that are needed to successfully defend your positions. In order to win the debate, you don't just need more facts than someone else, you also need to understand how to tactfully deconstruct a poorly formed argument.

Hunting is very important and special to me. It is a core component of our country's history and a foundational element to what it means to be an American. Hunting has helped me to grow as a person, learn critical life skills, and connect with God's creation. I hope that by reading this book you walk away better informed, prepared, and inspired to defend your positions against those who wish harm upon our way of life.

I also hope that no matter what, you will educate yourself on the facts and stand up for what you believe in, even when it is difficult. The individual freedoms that we enjoy are a uniquely American blessing. We must do everything in our power to defend those freedoms now and in the future. It is my hope that this book will offer a deeper understanding of the history, the significance, and the practical implications of the Second Amendment in our country today. In a world with so much information -- and so much misinformation -- it's important to reflect on the basics and arm yourself with facts.

Why Do We Have The Second Amendment?

A few years back I was speaking to a group of students on a college campus, and the Second Amendment was brought up during Q&A. A student said "Charlie, I support the right to bear arms and I want to defend it, but I don't know how to respond when my peers say that we don't need guns because we have a well-trained military now. The Second Amendment says that militias have the right to bear arms, but not average citizens. How do I refute that?"

The question kind of shocked me because it was the first time I realized that even people who support the Second Amendment don't understand why we have it. I don't blame the student for not knowing this, but I do blame our education system. It's a horribly sad fact that we live in a country where people who go to college still don't understand why we have the rights and freedoms that are included in the U.S. Constitution.

In order to understand why we need the Second Amendment today, we must first understand why it was included in our Constitution in the first place.

Before we dive into the reasoning behind it, I want to address what exactly the Second Amendment says and what the Founders meant by it. Bear with me if this seems overly basic; specifics matter here. With proper research and interpretation, it is very easy to understand what the Founders intended and why they included this critically important right.

The Second Amendment to the U.S. Constitution, which guarantees the right for citizens to keep and bear arms, reads as follows:

> *"A well regulated militia, being necessary to the security of a free State, the right of the people to keep and bear Arms, shall not be infringed."*

Some people believe that the Second Amendment must only applies to organized forces like the military because it says "a well regulated militia" has the right to keep and bear arms. They believe that this terminology excludes the average citizen and provides a right only for a force that is overseen and maintained (or "regulated") by our government. This argument, while sometimes common, is rooted in a deep failure to understand the meaning of the words used by our Founding Fathers.

In 2012 *The Daily Kos* posted:

> "Until this so-called militia is being adequately regulated, the purported right of the people to keep and bear arms MUST be infringed. If it is not regulated (or infringed upon), such a militia actually undermines and threatens the security of the state."
>
> *The Daily Kos, December 25, 2012*

To breakdown this argument, let's first take a look at what the Founding Fathers meant when they used the term "militia." It's important that we understand their terms and their language as we interpret their intentions.

When the Founding Fathers were drafting the Constitution, every town had a militia. These militias were not groups of extensively vetted and well-trained infantrymen, but rather were made up of every able-bodied man in the town. It was not a selective service, but rather a force made up of everyone who owned a gun and was able to walk. Despite what gun control advocates try to make you think, a militia was just a group of everyday individuals.

The Daily Kos continued by saying, "the best case for gun control was made in the Second Amendment. After all, it says they (guns) should be regulated."

Now, let's analyze what the Founding Fathers meant when they wrote, "well-regulated." While some believe that " a well regulated militia" means that the militia must be controlled and overseen by the state, the Founders had a much different understanding of the word.

During the time that the Founders were drafting the Constitution, the Oxford Dictionary defined "regulated" as something that was "well calibrated and functioning as expected." If we apply that definition to the Second Amendment, it would suggest that the Founding Fathers were calling for a high-functioning, well-prepared, and well-run group -- not a state-controlled force. Regulated had nothing to do with rules or guidelines; it had everything to do with something being in proper working order.

Today, the dictionary defines "regulate" as "to control or supervise (something, especially a company or business activity) by means of rules and regulations by means of rules and regulations." This is a much different definition than the one applied by the Founding Fathers.

As you can see, it is important to evaluate the meaning of the words used when analyzing historical documents. The meanings of words can change over time, and we need to account for that. For example, the word "awful" used to mean "worthy of awe." Today, we use the term to describe things that are bad and unpleasant. The word "nice" used to mean silly, foolish, or simple. Today, it's considered a compliment.[1] The meaning of words changes all the time, and it would be intellectually irresponsible to fail to account for that.

The Founding Fathers clarified their intent in other documents, too. In Federalist Paper Number 46, James Madison, the author of the Bill of Rights, wrote, "The ultimate authority resides in the people, and if the federal government got too powerful and overstepped its authority then the people would develop plans of resistance and resort to arms."

James Madison makes it very clear in this elaboration of the Second Amendment that it is not about giving government the ability to possess arms, but rather "the people." The fundamental purpose is to resist government tyranny, and provide the common people with the ability to protect their freedoms, liberties, and natural rights.

The answer to "why" we have the Second Amendment is well-articulated by the Founding Fathers. In my view, there really isn't a lot of room to debate this. When we analyze their words and look to their own defenses of the Second Amendment, the meaning and intent is crystal clear. **They gave us the Second Amendment so that we could defend ourselves from government should it ever become tyrannical.**

Of course, some people will still argue that while the Founding Fathers may have included the Second Amendment to protect ourselves from tyranny, this right is outdated because tyrannical governments are no longer a serious possibility or threat. I wholeheartedly disagree with that argument and will refute it at length later in this book.

---

[1] https://ideas.ted.com/20-words-that-once-meant-something-very-different/

There are many examples of tyrannical governments that emerged after the founding of the United States -- and it's no coincidence that these governments became oppressive only after the citizens were disarmed.

Another argument I hear is that the Second Amendment was intended to give us the right to self-defense, but we don't need that anymore because of our military and advanced police forces. That logic is flawed on many levels, all of which I'll discuss at length, but the most important point is that the Founders weren't really concerned about self-defense. To them, self-defense was a benefit but not the purpose of the Second Amendment. Their primary concern was about the people maintaining control of their government and being capable of resisting oppression and tyranny.

There is also a crowd that believes that the Second Amendment is dangerous to the public, and therefore needs to be eliminated or at least greatly restricted in the name of public safety. This, too, is a deeply flawed argument with no factual evidence to support it. It is true that guns can be used as deadly weapons, but more often than not they are used to defend an innocent person or group of people from harm. More important than that use, however, firearms serve as a safeguard for our liberties and freedoms. Sacrificing our rights and freedoms while also taking away our right to self-defense would be extremely counter-productive.

While I disagree with the anti-gun arguments, I believe that most people's concerns about the Second Amendment stem not from bad intentions but rather from exposure to misinformation. I truly believe that the average person who opposes the Second Amendment is both educated and well-meaning. Whenever I debate people on this topic, I find that my opponents frequently come armed with facts, figures, and statistics to back-up their points. I don't doubt that they did their research and believe in what they're saying; I doubt their sources. There is a lot of information out there, but *a lot of it is highly misleading or completely inaccurate*. The internet, the mainstream media, and social media are full of articles, videos, and reports that make completely false claims. It's no surprise that people are so confused on this issue.

While the average person who supports gun control measures is probably well-intentioned and genuinely convinced that their policy position would produce value, they are being misled. I don't fully blame them for being misinformed, but I do blame the people doing the misinforming.

Make no mistake -- there is a concerted and well-planned effort by folks on the left to advance their gun control agenda at all costs. The biggest cultural influencers from the mainstream media and social media to Hollywood and college professors are doing everything in their power to take away our Second Amendment. To them, it's not about guns; it's about control. Guns make people inherently less dependent on government. When the people aren't armed, they turn to their government for protection. Leftists want the government to be the only entity capable of helping people, so that people remain dependent on it. They're terrified of people being free and not needing them.

These people on the left know exactly what they're doing. They politicize tragedies, promote propaganda, and ignore any facts that don't fit their narrative. Most tragically, they don't seem to care about the devastating implications of their tried and failed gun control policies. Democrats have run Chicago for more than eight decades and implemented some of the toughest gun control laws in our country. Despite those efforts, Chicago is experiencing record-breaking gun violence, and nothing is changing. The left doesn't seem to care. They protest guns while being surrounded by armed guards.[2] They call for gun control and gun-free zones, then enroll their children in schools that are protected by armed guards. The hypocrisy is real, and they know it. The right to bear arms puts power in the hands of the people. The Founding Fathers wrote the Second Amendment so that "We The People" could hold our government accountable and resist a tyrannical and oppressive government should it arise.

Once you understand why we have the Second Amendment, you understand why we need it *now more than ever*. Tyrannical governments can and do emerge, and America was founded on the notion that "We The People" are responsible for holding our government in check. If you infringe upon that right, you infringe upon your very own freedom, liberty, and life. People who run for elected Federal positions have an obligation to defend the Constitution and our rights as they are and should be questioned on this before we vote for them.

The answer to why we have the Second Amendment is something that I hope every American considers throughout their lifetime. So many people throughout the world never have the opportunity to experience or benefit from the rights and privileges we have in the United States. We have an obligation to understand and appreciate the rights we've been given.

---

[2] http://www.theblaze.com/news/2017/07/15/liberal-feminist-women-spent-day-protesting-nra-but-their-leaders-walked-around-with-armed-guards/

What Was The Founders' Intent?

The Founding Fathers were very intentional about how they wrote the United States Constitution. They were adamant about setting up a system of government that would protect current and future citizens from the rise of an overpowering, out-of-control, possibly tyrannical government. They debated, discussed, and revised the document several times before presenting a final product. It took 116 days to draft the U.S. Constitution.

As I discussed in the previous chapter, the language of the Founders -- both in the Second Amendment itself and in other philosophical documents -- points to a clear purpose. **The Founding Fathers included the Second Amendment so that citizens could defend themselves from government should it ever become tyrannical and infringe upon their natural rights.**

They intended for a well-regulated militia (meaning a high-functioning, well-prepared group of average, able-bodied citizens) to have the right to possess a firearm. If you doubt this, look no further than Federalist Paper Number 46 in which James Madison, the author of the Bill of Rights, explained, "...if the federal government got too powerful and overstepped its authority then the people would develop plans of resistance and resort to arms."

The concept of natural rights, the very thing that the Second Amendment was designed to protect, was discussed in the Declaration of Independence. The beginning of the document reads:

> We hold these truths to be self-evident, that all men are created equal, that they are endowed by their

Creator with certain **unalienable Rights**, *that among these are Life, Liberty and the pursuit of Happiness. — That to secure these rights, Governments are instituted among Men, deriving their just powers from the consent of the governed, — That whenever any Form of Government becomes destructive of these ends, it is the Right of the People to alter or to abolish it, and to institute new Government, laying its foundation on such principles and organizing its powers in such form, as to them shall seem most likely to effect their Safety and Happiness.*

In the Founders' view, the Second Amendment ensured that our unalienable rights would be protected. The logic here is quite simple. You have the right to life, but how can you defend that without the Second Amendment? You have the right to liberty (as opposed to tyranny), but how can you defend that without the Second Amendment? If the people cannot hold their government accountable, the people have no real power. The governed live at the mercy of the government, and that goes against everything the Founding Fathers believed in, fought for, and in many cases died for.

We know what the Founding Fathers thought, but what about the people?

The U.S. Constitution was signed by 38 of the 41 delegates present at the Constitutional Convention in Philadelphia. Supporters of the new constitution had to put up a strong fight to secure ratification by the necessary nine out of 13 U.S. states. They had to listen to the people -- a uniquely American idea -- and craft a document that they believed in and would support.

The version of the U.S. Constitution that was signed on September 17, 1787 did not include the Second Amendment, or any amendments at all. The Bill of Rights, which is comprised of the first 10 amendments, was added over a year later in response to strict demands from the states for greater protections from the federal government.

During the ratification process for our U.S. Constitution, many state conventions called for the addition of amendments that specifically protected individual rights and personal liberties from an overreaching federal government. By June of 1788, 9 states had ratified the Constitution, but key states including Virginia and New York had not agreed to do so. James Madison, the primary author of our Constitution, knew that this document would not be widely accepted if Virginia and New York did not adopt it. Madison himself was from Virginia, as were many of the Constitution's chief architects.

During the ratification debate in Virginia, James Madison promised that a bill of rights would be added after ratification. His promise was reassuring to the people, and the Constitution was narrowly ratified by Virginia shortly after. New York soon followed. Rhode Island and North Carolina, however, refused to ratify without the addition of a bill of rights. A year later, in June of 1789, Madison proposed a series of amendments known as the Bill of Rights to be debated in the first Congress. North Carolina then ratified the Constitution in 1789, and Rhode Island became the 13th and final state to ratify and join the union in May of 1790.

History tells us that the U.S. Constitution probably wouldn't have been ratified without the addition of the Bill of Rights. **The protections from government were *that* important.**

The Bill of Rights were designed specifically to limit the power of the federal government. The fear of an oppressive, tyrannical, and out of control government was real. The founders understood that without proper planning and effective boundaries, tyranny could emerge and the people would suffer. Every amendment found in the Bill of Rights gives us a protection *from* government, and the Second Amendment was designed to be no different. Let's look at the other amendments and examine exactly how they protect us.

The location of this amendment within the Constitution tells us a lot about its meaning. The Second Amendment is found in the Bill of Rights, which contains a list of liberties that protect the people *from* their government. Every single one of the amendments in the Bill of Rights -- from the first to the tenth -- gives *us* a freedom *from* our federal government. The Second Amendment is no different.

The First Amendment - Congress shall make no law respecting an establishment of religion, or prohibiting the free exercise thereof; or abridging the freedom of speech, or of the press; or the right of the people peaceably to assemble, and to petition the government for a redress of grievances.

This amendment protects us from persecution from our government based on our speech and our religion. It also protects our right to a press that isn't regulated by the government, and our right to petition or assemble against our government when we disagree with it.

The first amendment does not protect us from criticism, the right to say whatever we want at work, or other negative repercussions from private citizens. Your private employer can fire you for saying something that they happen to find offensive. The first amendment only guarantees that your **government** cannot persecute you for what you say. Of course, tolerance is about respecting free speech and allowing a wide variety of thoughts to coexist in peace, but the Constitution does not require tolerance from private citizens.

For now, I'm going to skip the Second Amendment. We'll get back to that shortly.

The Third Amendment - No soldier shall, in time of peace be quartered in any house, without the consent of the owner, nor in time of war, but in a manner to be prescribed by law.

This amendment protects us from the government forcing soldiers into our homes. Like the first amendment, the third amendment specifically protects us from government-inflicted harm.

The Fourth Amendment - The right of the people to be secure in their persons, houses, papers, and effects, against unreasonable searches and seizures, shall not be violated, and no warrants shall issue, but upon probable cause, supported by oath or affirmation, and particularly describing the place to be searched, and the persons or things to be seized.

The fourth amendment protects us from the government searching our homes and our property without a warrant and a legitimate reason to search.

It doesn't mean that your private employer can't search your office, or that you have any right to privacy from your neighbors and fellow citizens. This particular amendment protects you only from the government.

The Fifth Amendment - No person shall be held to answer for a capital, or otherwise infamous crime, unless on a presentment or indictment of a grand jury, except in cases arising in the land or naval forces, or in the militia, when in actual service in time of war or public danger; nor shall any person be subject for the same offense to be twice put in jeopardy of life or limb; nor shall be compelled in any criminal case to be a witness against himself, nor be deprived of life, liberty, or property, without due process of law; nor shall private property be taken for public use, without just compensation.

The Fifth Amendment gives us a wide variety of protections from our government when we are being charged with a crime. It protects us from being tried by the government without a Grand Jury finding sufficient evidence against us. It also protects us from being tried twice for the same crime, being forced to admit our own guilt, and being forced to testify against ourselves. This amendment also states that we cannot be punished by our government (killed, put in jail, etc.) without all of the proper legal steps being followed, and it protects us from the government taking our property without payment at a fair price.

The Sixth Amendment - In all criminal prosecutions, the accused shall enjoy the right to a speedy and public trial, by an impartial jury of the state and district wherein the crime shall have been committed, which district shall have been previously ascertained by law, and to be informed of the nature and cause of the accusation; to be confronted with the witnesses against him; to have compulsory process for obtaining witnesses in his favor, and to have the assistance of counsel for his defense.

This amendment gives us the right to a fair and speedy trial when our government charges us with a crime. It also protects us from the government holding us in jail for no cause or holding us for a crime without telling us what we're accused of doing wrong. It also establishes the right to a trial by jury in criminal cases.

The Seventh Amendment - In suits at common law, where the value in controversy shall exceed twenty dollars, the right of trial by jury shall be preserved, and no fact tried by a jury, shall be otherwise reexamined in any court of the United States, than according to the rules of the common law.

This amendment gives us the right to a trial by jury in civil cases. While civil cases are cases between two people (rather than one person and the government), this amendment still protects us from the government overturning a jury's findings for no reason.

The Eighth Amendment - Excessive bail shall not be required, nor excessive fines imposed, nor cruel and unusual punishments inflicted.

This amendment protects us from cruel and unusual punishment (such as torture) from our government, even if we are convicted of a crime. This amendment also protects us from unreasonably high bail and fines imposed by the government.

The Eighth amendment is not about a protection from cruel and unusual punishment in general. It doesn't have anything to do with punishments at work, or parents spanking their kids as a form of punishment (of course, other laws could be and have been created to address these types of things). Like the other amendments we've reviewed so far, the eighth amendment is about protecting us specifically from *government-inflicted* harm.

The Ninth Amendment - The enumeration in the Constitution, of certain rights, shall not be construed to deny or disparage others retained by the people.

This amendment gives us (the people) the ability to assume rights that are not specifically listed in the Constitution. This amendment protects us from the government denying us a right that isn't spelled out.

The Tenth Amendment - The powers not delegated to the United States by the Constitution, nor prohibited by it to the states, are reserved to the states respectively, or to the people.

The tenth amendment protects us from the federal government assuming a new power or authority that is not specifically mentioned in the Constitution. This amendment limits the power of the federal government to functions that are specifically enumerated and nothing more.

As you can see, every single amendment in the Bill of Rights gives us a protection *from* our federal government.

The Second Amendment is no different. It reads:

"A well regulated militia, being necessary to the security of a free State, the right of the people to keep and bear Arms, shall not be infringed."

The Second Amendment protects us from government-inflicted harm. It levels the playing field between the people and the people in power by giving every citizen the right and ability to challenge an oppressive, tyrannical government.

The Bill of Rights, including the Second Amendment, were insisted upon by the states. It was well agreed upon by nearly all early Americans that the right for citizens to bear arms should be protected.

Understanding Tyrannical Government

"Experience hath shewn, that even under the best forms of government those entrusted with power have, in time, and by slow operations, perverted it into tyranny."
-Thomas Jefferson

When you think of real-world tyrannical governments, leaders like Maximilien Robespierre, Joseph Stalin, Adolf Hitler, Pol Pot, and a handful of others probably come to mind. It's a well-accepted fact that tyranny has existed, and in some places across the world still exists today.

The Merriam-Webster dictionary defines "tyranny" as "oppressive power, especially oppressive power exerted by government."[3] In short, tyranny is cruel and oppressive government.

The Founding Fathers were terrified of tyranny. They understood, having lived through it themselves, that large federal governments **can and do** oppress their own citizens. They learned from experience that concentrated power is dangerous, and liberty must be consistently defended and preserved.

It was not lost on the Founding Fathers that many of their ancestors came to America to escape tyranny -- most commonly in the form of religious persecution. The first American colonies were founded by people who refused to conform to their state's religion and sought a place to worship God in the way they believed to be correct.

---

[3] https://www.merriam-webster.com/dictionary/tyranny

They also lived through the American Revolution -- a battle that began because government got too big, too demanding, and too oppressive.

All of these experiences led the Founders to be extremely mindful and fearful of tyranny. Their vision for America was to create a place that protected each person's God-given natural rights, and they knew that an overreaching, oppressive government would pose a major threat to life, liberty, and freedom.

Throughout the U.S. Constitution you will find numerous examples of the Founding Fathers' deep desire for a small, limited, and controlled federal government. Below are a few examples to demonstrate my point:

Separation of Powers
The founders set-up a federal government that is divided into three branches: the legislative, the executive, and the judicial.

Checks and Balances
Each of the three branches of government has robust checks and balances on the others. This prevents one branch from becoming tyrannical.

Enumerated Powers
The founders specifically limited the federal government's power to the powers specifically stated in the Constitution. The government cannot assume any additional powers without permission from the people.

Power To The States and The People

The founders ensured that any authority that is not specifically given to the federal government is reserved for the states and the people. When in doubt, the people are in power.

As you can see, the Founding Fathers were very intentional about limiting the federal government. The fear of tyranny was real. The Second Amendment, which gave the people the power to defend themselves against their government, is an important part of preventing oppression and fighting tyranny should it arise.

Some people argue that tyrannical governments couldn't exist today. I will argue that too many people have paid too high a price for giving government the benefit of the doubt. The horrors that took place in Nazi Germany offer a good example.

In 1931, the Weimar authorities discovered plans for an upcoming Nazi takeover. The plans specified that the Jews would be denied food and water, and anyone who refused to surrender their guns within 24 hours would be executed. As a response to these threats, the government authorized a statewide registration of all firearms, and promised to confiscate all firearms if required for "public safety."

In 1933, Adolf Hitler came into power and used these pre-established records to identify and disarm Jews and anyone who sided with them. Constitutional rights were suspended, and the government organized extensive searches for guns. The police revoked gun licenses from anyone who was not "politically reliable."

Throughout the next few years, Hitler and the National Socialist regime used their power to "cleanse" society of everyone they found undesirable. Citizens were forced into labor camps. Jews were put to death in gas chambers. It was horrific, but no one could stop them.

The gun registry, which perhaps started with good intentions, ultimately took away millions of people's ability to defend themselves. While painful to think about, the death toll in Nazi Germany might have been a lot lower if the people had the right to bear arms and resist the tyranny that emerged in their country. Sadly, the people had no defense against the state. They were sitting ducks. This happened less than 100 years ago, and I would argue that it could happen again 100 years from now. There are evil people, and sometimes those evil people come into power, and risking the formation of another Nazi Germany isn't a risk I'm willing to take.

Freedom isn't guaranteed, but our best chance at preserving it is maintaining the power to resist our government should it ever become oppressive. The Second Amendment makes that possible in America, and it is part of the reason why our system of government is so admired and looked up to throughout the world.

Putting Power Back In The Hands Of The People

"It's not tyranny we desire; it's a just, limited, federal government."
-Alexander Hamilton

The Founding Fathers wanted to create a system of government that put power in the hands of the people. Since the beginning of our nation, this concept has been admired, replicated, and fought for by millions of people throughout the world.

With this goal in mind, the Founding Fathers crafted a Constitution that would protect and preserve a government of the people, by the people, and for the people. They were intentional about their approach and took numerous measures to limit the power of the federal government to very specific functions. The Second Amendment was one of those measures. It gave us, the citizens, the ability to maintain the same power and force as the state and protect ourselves against any direct threats or oppressive governments.

The Second Amendment is one of the most important aspects of securing power for the people. I would argue that without the Second Amendment, all of the other freedoms and liberties we have could very quickly cease to exist. How do we have the freedom to say what we want if we cannot defend ourselves against a government that persecutes us? How can we protect our freedom to choose our own religion if we don't have any ability to challenge a government that infringes upon that? How can we protect our natural rights if our government decides to violate them? The answer to all of these questions is that without the Second Amendment, we can't.

In order for people to be free, they must have unrestricted ability to bear arms.

Some people argue that certain types of guns are acceptable for self-defense, but others are too powerful or too dangerous. While I'm sure these people are well-intentioned and are hoping only to make the world a safer place, there is a fundamental flaw with their logic.

The Second Amendment specified that we have the right to bear arms. There were no specific types of arms mentioned. The Founding Fathers understood that while technology may change evolve over time, our rights are permanent. They wanted the American people to have the right to access whatever arms were available at the time, not necessarily a specific type of gun.

The Constitution wasn't written for the times, but rather it was written to stand the test of time. Understanding this concept is an important part of understanding what it means to give political power to the people. Without the ability to the defend oneself from government and hold the people with power in check, there is no freedom or liberty.

If you believe in freedom, liberty, and the idea that "We The People" should be in charge of our government, it's essential that you support the Second Amendment. The Second Amendment protects the other 26 amendments.

Using a weapon isn't what makes you free; freedom lies in the power to successfully defend yourself when harmful forces come your way. You won't see Second Amendment supporters advocating that we use firearms on a daily basis.

That isn't their objective. What Second Amendment advocates fight for is the *right* to own and carry a weapon and use it only when a legitimate need exists.

It's no surprise that the least free societies in the world have banned guns. Oppressive governments are deeply threatened by citizens who possess the power to fight back. During the Revolutionary War, the British tried to limit the continuation of anything that advanced American independence and freedom. They implemented restrictions on guns and ammunition destined for the American colonies. They did not want to empower local militias that might pose a threat. The Founding Fathers understood this very simple truth: guns keep you free.

Protecting the Second Amendment goes hand in hand with protecting freedom. It gives us the right to protect ourselves and our families from harm and hold our government in check should it ever become tyrannical. If you believe in putting power in the hands of the people, you have to believe in supporting the Second Amendment.

Explaining Our Hunting Heritage

Hunting is a very popular activity in which nearly every society throughout history of the world has participated. Recently discovered evidence suggests that our early human ancestors began hunting over 2 million years ago.[4] Hunting is one of the oldest and most common human traditions.

Estimates show that there are over 13.7 million hunters in the United States today. [5] That's a lot of people! The population of hunters in just four states -- Wisconsin, Pennsylvania, Michigan, and West Virginia -- would outnumber the world's largest army.[6] According to the National Survey of Fishing Hunting and Wildlife-Associated Recreation, there are around 90.1 million Americans that enjoys hunting, fishing, and wildlife recreation. This figure amounts to 38% of the total population of the United States.[7] Everyone knows someone who hunts. The hunting community is made up of millions of men, women, and children who live in every corner of our country.

Like the Second Amendment, hunting is often attacked by the left. The arguments range from suggesting that hunting is dangerous to portraying hunters as evil, bloodthirsty people

---

[4] https://www.livescience.com/31974-earliest-human-hunters-found.html

[5] https://wsfrprograms.fws.gov/subpages/nationalsurvey/2011_Survey.htm

[6] http://nation.foxnews.com/2013/11/04/american-hunters-%E2%80%93-world%E2%80%99s-largest-army

[7] https://huntingtopics.com/many-people-in-the-us-hunt/

who don't care about animals or the environment. The truth is that hunting is a very safe sport, and hunters are some of the most generous, conscientious, conservation-minded people that I know. There is a lot of evidence to demonstrate that hunters do more than any other group -- including the government -- for animals, wildlife, and our natural resources. Most attacks on hunting as well as the hunting community are illogical and downright wrong.

Hunting isn't for everyone, and I'm not here to convince you to take up hunting if it doesn't interest you. My hope is to help you understand what hunting is all about, and why so many people enjoy doing it. Regardless of whether or not you participate, I believe there is still value in knowing the history of the sport and what it means to the hunting community. If you do hunt, I hope to offer facts and examples that will help you defend our hunting heritage and spread the truth about hunting with facts, examples, and strong points.

What are the positives of hunting?

Hunting has an overwhelmingly positive impact on people, their communities, and the world. The Left tries their best to portray hunting as a negative, dangerous, and harmful activity that poses a threat to people, animals, and the environment. The truth is that hunting's positive impact reaches far beyond the hunting community.

I discuss a lot of these benefits at length in other places throughout the book, but I feel that it's important to include a complete summary. My hope is that this list will prove helpful to you as you reflect on the impact of hunting and educate others about the hunting community.

Economic Benefits
- The hunting industry sustains over 680,000 jobs in America,[8] and generates over $17 billion in salaries and wages.[9] This creates job opportunities for hundreds of thousands of citizens as well as income tax revenue for federal and state governments. Income tax revenue generated by hunters is estimated to be over $2.4 billion.[10]
- The hunting industry generates over $25 billion in retail sales each year, which sustains

---

[8]http://www.rmef.org/Conservation/HuntingIsConservation/25 ReasonsWhyHuntingIsConservation.aspx

[9] http://www.fishwildlife.org/files/Hunting_Economic_Impact.pdf

[10] http://www.fishwildlife.org/files/Hunting_Economic_Impact.pdf

retail jobs and generates a significant amount of sales tax revenue.[11]

- The hunting community supports industries that have nothing to do with hunting. Each year hunters spend more money on food for hunting trips than Americans collectively spend on Domino's pizza.[12] Hunters also spend over $605 million per year on their hunting dogs.

Environmental Benefits

- Every single day U.S. sportsmen contribute $8 million to conservation.
- Through state licenses and hunting-related fees, hunters contribute over $796 million per year for conservation programs in the United States.
- An 11% tax that hunters pay on guns, ammo, bows and arrows generates $371 million a year for conservation.[13]

Personal Benefits

- For many people hunting is a relaxing and enjoyable recreational activity. It offers hunters a chance to clear their mind while doing something they enjoy.

---

[11] http://www.fishwildlife.org/files/Hunting_Economic_Impact.pdf
[12] http://www.fishwildlife.org/files/Hunting_Economic_Impact.pdf
[13] http://www.rmef.org/Conservation/HuntingIsConservation/25 ReasonsWhyHuntingIsConservation.aspx

- Hunting offers unique and highly valuable educational opportunities that teach people about gun safety, sportsmanship, wildlife, nature, and conservation.
- Hunting is one of the safest recreational activities in which a person can participate. It is a much safer alternative to the most common sports that children play such a soccer, football, and baseball.

As you can see, hunting offers a wide range of benefits to the people who hunt, as well as the communities in which people hunt and our country as a whole.

Our Approach to Controversial Issues

It's no secret that we live in a very divided world. When it comes to issues like gun control, everyone has an opinion and those opinions are held in high regard. There's nothing inherently wrong with believing in something strongly; in fact, I started an organization that encourages people to do that. The problem begins when we become unwilling to have civil discussions with people who don't see the issues our way.

Sadly, I believe we're living in a time in which many people are unwilling and unable to have open, honest, and productive discussions about the most pressing issues of our times. This is concerning because the only way to grow our movement and spread our ideas is to talk about them in an open setting. I blame our culture for this trend. From higher education to Hollywood to the mainstream media, the people who influence millions of minds are making us more intolerant by the minute.

For example, during the 2016 Presidential campaign, filmmaker Michael Moore proclaimed that all Trump supporters were racists. His exact quote was, "If you still support the racist, you are the racist.[14]" This is just one example of someone making a very broad, overarching character assessment about a group of people based on one opinion they hold – in this case, an opinion about who to support for President of the United States. This behavior is incredibly intolerant and leads to people either following the

---

[14] http://variety.com/2017/legit/news/michael-moore-cnn-interview-trump-racist-1202529456/

example set by our culture or disengaging from the discussion altogether.

Some people create and exert "us vs. them" mentalities and actions which make many people afraid and hesitant to say what they think and believe in response. I'm all for people saying what they want, and I'll defend the first amendment even when I don't like what is being said, but if our goal is to make progress on pressing issues we need to create a culture in which people are comfortable and capable of speaking openly with one another.

If you've ever come across a political post on Facebook, you know it's common to see "comment wars" breakout in the comments section. I recently saw someone share a gun control meme and was shocked to see over a dozen comments calling the person everything from an incompetent idiot to an uneducated and defective moron. Sure, you can say that and I'll defend your right to say it every single day, but what does it accomplish if you're actually concerned about the gun control issue? Does it make people want to think your way, or does it make people afraid to engage in this debate at all? I'd argue the latter.

When politics gets personal and hurtful, it turns people off. I recently spoke to a high school student who believes in freedom, liberty, and the Second Amendment. I asked him if he would like to get involved with Turning Point USA – the organization I founded to advance limited government on college campuses. He said, "I believe those things, but politics doesn't interest me. It's just too nasty for me." The hate, the intolerance, and negativity turn good people away from advancing our ideas and being part of this important cause. Both sides are to blame for this. I believe that our approach to controversial issues is all wrong.

As people who understand and appreciate the Second Amendment, we must recognize the need to get more people on board for our ideas. The future of the Second Amendment depends on citizens protecting and preserving it. We need to embrace people who create opportunities for open, honest, and candid discussions. We need to approach discussions with respect, maturity, and seriousness, and always remember that people are watching. Our approach and our attitude will impact the way outsiders and onlookers perceive our ideas. We need to create a culture that incentivizes participation, interest, and respectful discussion.

The good news is that we have the facts on our side. We do not need to resort to name-calling and personal attacks. We have what it takes to win any debate. There is statistic after statistic to prove the value of the Second Amendment. We must simply be leaders and initiators of fruitful and open-minded discussion. We must welcome debates, honest conversations, and sincere disagreements. It is through these conversations that people will learn more of the true meaning of the Second Amendment.

It is important for me to reiterate that I'm not against exposing false claims and pointing out the hypocrisy and irrational arguments. I do this all the time when I'm debating leftists in person or social media, and I think it is an effective way of opening people's eyes to new points of view. Asking difficult questions and expecting people to defend their ideas is not only acceptable but essential. It is our approach that matters.

We need to discuss issues with respect, maturity, and seriousness. In practice, that means remaining calm, listening to the other perspective, using a sincere and kind tone, and refraining from personal attacks and sarcastic remarks. We need to be able to see something we disagree with on Facebook, and either ignore it or respectfully share our opinion rather than report the post and call the person who shared it an idiot. The left likes to eliminate things they disagree with – we cannot let that happen in our movement.

I am an outspoken advocate for standing up for correct beliefs. I founded an organization that is dedicated to identifying, training, and empowering young people to stand up for what they believe in and fighting fearlessly for the advancement of their ideas. You will never hear me say that we should not be bold advocates for the causes we support, or that we should not expose hypocrisy, inaccuracies, or injustices when we see them. I believe it is our duty – to ourselves and to each other – to seek the truth and help as many people as possible see and understand that truth, too.

My point is about approach. We need to be willing and able to have discussions with people who don't see things our way. We need to be open-minded enough to see that they can be good-hearted, well-meaning, and well-educated, too. We cannot get so caught up in our beliefs that we look down on people who disagree with us. The only way we'll grow our movement and advance our ideas is through effective, articulate, and candid discussion. We are brand reps for our ideas, and whether we like it or not our approach and our attitude influence the way other people perceive our philosophy.

You do not have to like the way a person thinks, and you definitely do not have to agree with them, but in order to be effective you really need to meet them in the middle and have a respectful, mature, and serious discussion.

5 Common Myths About Guns And The Second Amendment

Whenever I speak on a college campus I find that the Second Amendment sparks more debate and discussion than nearly any other issue.

Part of this is due to the highly emotional nature of the topic. It is a life or death issue. Gun deaths are devastating, and the price we pay for gun violence is significant. People on both sides of the issue believe that their policy prescription would accomplish a lot in terms of solving this problem, so understandably they are passionate about enacting it.

I also believe this issue is controversial because it's about so much more than guns. It's about freedom, liberty, and the right to self-defense. It's also about power, influence, and control. The Second Amendment has very broad implications on our lives and livelihood, and for that reason this issue tops the charts in terms of importance.

The facts about gun control point clearly in one direction, but the facts aren't always well articulated. There are so many misconceptions and misunderstandings about guns in America. We owe it to ourselves and to each other to correct them.

Most everyone agrees on the goal. Gun control advocates want less crime and more safety. **I share their goal,** and I believe that most people who engage in debates about guns truly want the same things. That said, I also believe in Milton Friedman's wise words:

"One of the great mistakes is to judge policies and programs by their intentions rather than their results."

To me, the facts on this issue are crystal clear. The ability to carry a gun and defend oneself can make the difference between living or dying. *It is the difference between being free to save your own life or depending on the government to do it for you. It is the difference between letting your government oppress you or defending your natural, God-given rights that so many before us died for.*

When discussing any issue, particularly those that can have a life or death impact, it is important to remain grounded in the facts. Facts are facts. Reality is reality. We must do our part to make sure that the facts are communicated in a clear, relatable, and widespread way.

I designed this section to be a tool used for changing minds and hearts on the Second Amendment. By citing facts, statistical evidence, and real-life examples, it is my hope that these next few chapters will help you see the truth about guns and the Second Amendment.

The Second Amendment is outdated.

Some people argue that the Second Amendment is outdated. Generally speaking, these people believe that while Americans may have once needed a weapon to protect themselves from the government or other citizens, they don't need one anymore.

This thinking concerns me. In the Second Amendment we have protection *from* our government. This protection was insisted upon by our Founding Fathers because they feared the rise of tyranny. Surrendering the right to self-defense means that you are giving up your right to defend yourself and depending on the government to do it for you. I don't know about you, but I don't want the same government that can't manage a DMV to be responsible for protecting my life. More importantly, what happens if it's the government that we want to defend ourselves against?

A 2016 Gallup poll showed us that a majority of Americans "don't trust the government."[15] If you don't trust your government, you certainly shouldn't want to make it bigger and give it more power over you. You also shouldn't want to give up your only method of protection against that government if it became oppressive and tyrannical.

When I speak on college campuses I always ask students, "Do you trust the government?" No matter where I ask this, the answer is overwhelmingly negative. Students from all political ideologies -- right, left, in the middle, and apathetic -- will admit that they do not trust the people in power. I follow up the first question with, "Do you think government is

---

[15] http://www.gallup.com/poll/5392/trust-government.aspx

becoming more or less trustworthy?" The common response is that students think it's getting worse. Most students that I talk to genuinely believe that government is less trustworthy today than it was 20 or 50 or 100 years ago. If that is the case, we should be more concerned than ever about preserving the power we hold in the Second Amendment.

If you're not worried about tyranny (which you absolutely should be -- especially if you don't trust your government, but I will get to that later), there is still the issue of protecting yourself from other citizens. In the Second Amendment we have the right to defend ourselves from all types of harm. Are there still violent crimes like armed robberies? Home invasions? Rapes? Assaults? Murders? Of course. Every day, thousands of Americans find themselves in situations where they need to defend themselves from attackers and violent crimes. The left likes to argue that this is why we have a police force, but a quick look at crime statistics proves that the police cannot protect us from everything.

According to the FBI, in 2015 there were over 15,000 murders, over 90,000 rapes, and over 1,000,000 total violent crimes committed across our nation. If police or government were always effective at protecting us, none of that would've happened. As long as criminals are walking our streets, the need for self-defense exists. No one is forcing anyone to carry a gun, but people most certainly deserve the right to opt-in for self-defense if they choose to do so. When given the choice, many people do.

In America today, guns are used over 2.5 million times per year for self-defense, and as many as 200,000 women use a gun every year to defend themselves against sexual abuse.[16]

---

[16] Kleck and Gertz, "Armed Resistance to Crime," at 185.

If that many people are actively *using* their right to self-defense, it seems illogical to call that right outdated. No one is forcing anyone to carry a gun for self-defense, but millions of people are choosing to do so and that right must be protected. No one deserves to be attacked, raped, or killed. If there is anything an innocent person can do to stop that from happening, I am all for it.

I am not saying that the Constitution should never be changed. Abolishing slavery and giving women the right to vote are just a few examples of the many times our Constitution has desperately needed an update. I applaud the positive changes we have made over time that given additional (and well-deserved) rights to different groups of people. Each of these updates offered additions to our rights, not a restriction on them. Expanding freedom and liberty is a very good thing.

I am, however, very weary of any change that *takes power away* from the people and gives it back to the government. This is what gun control advocates strive to accomplish.

The U.S. Constitution was designed to give power to the citizens, and any effort to expand the government's power is a step in the wrong direction. When we take away the right to bear arms, we take away self-defense from law-abiding citizens and give criminals the upper hand.

Criminals don't follow laws. That's what makes them criminals. Until every person in America is a law-abiding citizen and violent crime permanently ceases to exist, and until there is no way for criminals to bring in guns from outside the U.S., there is a legitimate need for the right to self-defense in America.

There is a reason that a majority of mass shootings have taken place in gun-free zones. There is a reason that homicide rates are highest in the cities with the most strict gun control laws. When you take away law-abiding people's right to defend themselves, criminals feel more comfortable committing crimes.

A similar yet slightly different perspective some hold is that the Second Amendment is outdated because technology has changed, and the guns we have available today are not what the Founding Fathers meant when they said "arms."

The Founding Fathers gave us the right to "bear arms." They didn't specify the types of guns we could use, just like they didn't limit freedom of speech to words communicated by quill pens and printing presses. The Second Amendment was about power for the people, not about the weapon. The First Amendment is about freedom of expression, not mediums of communication. We need to be intellectually consistent. Technology changes, but rights do not.

Twitter didn't exist when the Constitution was drafted, but it goes without saying that you have the right to express yourself freely on this newly created means of communication. You can tweet out a criticism of your government without thinking twice because you know that you have a right to speak freely. People understand this logic when it comes to the first amendment, but not always when it comes to the second. Why is the same logic not applied to the right to bear arms? We were given the right to defend ourselves, so why does the weapon used matter? The truth is, it doesn't.

The Second Amendment was not about the weapon. It was about tyranny and the right to protect yourself.

Taking away rights is a slippery slope. America was founded on the idea that people – not government – should be in control. We were also founded on the idea that people have natural rights, and an inherent right to protect and preserve those natural rights at all costs. Deciding that a protection *from* our government and *from* harm is no longer needed is concerning to me, and it should be concerning to anyone who values freedom, liberty, and self-defense.

Key Points:
- Americans do not trust their government (and rightly so). It does not make sense to give up an essential protection *from* your government if you don't have faith in it. You cannot preserve liberty and freedom without the ability to defend yourself from a government that tries to take it away.
- Violent crimes are not a thing of the past. Robberies, rapes, murders, and other violent crimes are still taking place, and therefore, the need for self-defense still exists. Victims deserve a fighting chance.
- Just like the first amendment doesn't apply to specific mediums of communication like a printing press or a quill pen, the Second Amendment doesn't apply to specific types of firearms. Technology changes. Rights do not.

More gun control means lower crime.

Generally speaking, gun control advocates are in favor of laws that limit the sale, possession, and use of firearms. Their hope is that by passing legislation that makes it harder for someone to access or use a firearm, less crimes will be committed. While I share their wish for lower crime rates, I cannot find any facts that support their logic.

By definition, a criminal is someone who has broken a law. To become a criminal, one must make the choice to break a law. It is against the law to rob someone at gunpoint or kill someone with a gun, yet criminals do it anyway. **That is what makes them criminals.** Logic tells me that if someone is willing to rob someone at gunpoint, they won't pay much attention to a "Gun Free Zone" sign, but I will defer to real life statistics and examples.

In 1976, the District of Columbia passed gun control legislation that made it illegal for any citizen, except a police officer, to carry a firearm. The law allowed people who already owned guns to keep their firearms, provided that they were disassembled or bound by a trigger-lock. The trigger-lock could only be removed with explicit permission from the D.C. police. Essentially, private citizens could not use guns.

From 1976 to 1988, the D.C. homicide rate rose from 188 to 364. Since the ban was struck down by the Supreme Court in *District of Columbia v. Heller*, the homicide rate has steadily decreased. While there may have been other reasons for the homicide rate decreasing, it is clear that ending the gun ban did not result in more murders.

D.C. still has some of the strictest gun laws in the country and happens to be one of the most dangerous places to live, but this example shows us that implementing a gun ban only made matters worse.

Let's look at another example. Chicago is known for having some of the strictest gun control laws in the country. In 2016, Chicago had 762 murders, 3,550 shooting incidents, and 4,331 shooting victims. The state of Illinois passed new gun control measured in 2016, and in turn experienced record-high crime rates. 2016 was an especially bad year for crime in Chicago, but this has been a long-term problem.

Chicago's violent crime rate in 2014 was 903.8 per 100,000. Phoenix, Arizona, which happens to be located in a state with some of the least-restrictive gun laws in the United States, had a violent crime rate of 593.8 per 100,000. Once again the facts show us that gun bans are ineffective in reducing crime rates.

It's also important to note that a vast majority of all mass murders in the United States have taken place in gun free zones. The Crime Research Prevention Center reported that 98.4% of all mass shootings from 1950 to 2016 occurred in a gun free zone. While incredibly devastating, this discovery makes sense. If a criminal is going to commit a mass murder, he or she is going to target an area in which their chance of being stopped is the lowest. Mass murderers would expect that the chance of a "good guy" being armed with a gun in a gun free zone is low. Good guys follow the laws. Bad guys don't.

Piers Morgan once said, "In the last 30 years there have been 62 mass shootings. Not a single one has ever been thwarted by a civilian despite America being a heavily armed country."

There is a lot wrong with this statement. First, we must acknowledge that of course there were no mass shootings thwarted by a civilian because if there had been, those events wouldn't be called mass shootings. It is impossible for us to know how many deadly situations were avoided by armed civilians, but we do know that armed civilians stop crimes all the time.[17] Glenn Beck picked up on this horribly misleading quote and explained it like this, "It's like saying not a single one of the 32,367 traffic fatalities that occurred in 2011 was thwarted by seat belts or air bags or speed limits. Yeah - no kidding, that's why they are fatalities."

In addition to the misleading wording, there are two fundamental problems with Piers' argument. The first is that he fails to mention all of the ways guns have in fact prevented horrendous shootings from occurring in real instances where the perpetrator had intended to kill many people. Also, Piers fails to mention that many of these shootings happened in gun free zones or areas where people were not allowed to be armed or defend themselves.

The truth of the matter is that gun control laws have failed our country, and armed citizens have saved lives. Here a few examples of guns saving the good guys:

Internet Cafe Robbery
In 2012, 71-year-old Internet café customer saved dozens of lives when he fired his own gun at two men trying to rob the store[18] in Ocala, FL. Had no one been armed, who knows how long the victims

---

[17] https://www.americanrifleman.org/the-armed-citizen
[18] http://www.foxnews.com/us/2012/07/19/florida-customer-who-shot-suspects-during-internet-cafe-robbery-will-not-face.html

would've been waiting for help, or how many would have died because they were defenseless.

Sarah McKinley's Story

In 2011, a brave young mother named Sarah McKinley who had lost her husband to lung cancer just a week earlier saved the life of herself and her baby when she used her gun to take down two knife-wielding intruders who entered her home[19].

Prince Middle School Shooting

In 1997, Luke Woodham, a troubled teenager from Pearl, Mississippi, began a murderous spree when he stabbed and bludgeoned his mother to death. After killing his own mother, he stole her car and drove to Pearl High School.

Armed with a rifle hidden inside a large trench coat, Luke entered the school and started shooting fellow students, one of which was his former girlfriend. Seven other students were badly wounded.

Luke then left the high school with the intention of going to the local junior high school to continue his line of killings. While in the parking lot, a school administrator retrieved a .45 caliber semi-automatic pistol from his truck and shouted at Luke to stop. Woodham ignored the yelling and tried to get away in his car. The school administrator approached the car and pointed the .45 caliber at him through the

---

[19] http://abcnews.go.com/US/okla-woman-shoots-kills-intruder911-operators-shoot/story?id=15285605

windshield. Shocked by this, Woodham crashed into a pole and stayed there until authorities arrived.

When police arrived and arrested Luke, they found over 30 rounds in his pockets. There is no telling how many innocent lives were saved that day, but what we do know is that a brave man with a gun was able to save more children from dying.

I could share dozens of real-life examples like these. **You cannot deny these stories.** Giving citizens the right to carry a firearm does in fact saves lives. Allowing people the right to defend themselves when they are in danger is a good thing. In the wise words of Wayne LaPierre, "The only thing that stops a bad guy with a gun is a good guy with a gun."

It is important that we keep facts, statistics, and real-world examples at the center of this conversation. We owe it to ourselves and to each other to be intellectually honest about the impact of our gun laws. Like most people engaged in this debate, I want less crime and more safety. The facts are clear that more gun control equals more crime.

Key Points:
- More gun control leads to more crime.
- Lifting gun bans (and reducing gun control) doesn't lead to an increase in crime.
- The vast majority of all mass shootings from 1950 to 2016 took place in a gun-free zone.
- There are countless stories about times when guns have saved innocent lies.
- Laws won't stop criminals. Criminals, by definition, are people who choose to break a pre-existing law.

- New laws that restrict our access to guns will be followed by citizens, but not criminals, thus increasing our risk.

Guns are tools of murder.

Can guns be a tool used to commit a murder? Sure, and so can cars, trucks, buses, knives, hammers, plastic bags, and even a person's own hands. The list of possible murder weapons is almost never-ending.

Given that list, most reasonable people would agree that it would be impossible to eliminate *all* of the possible murder weapons that exist in our society. When a crazy person plows a car into a crowd of people, you don't see rallies of 'car-control' activists seeking a ban on cars. It's understood that while a car *could* be used to commit a murder, it isn't exclusively used for that purpose – and cars do more good than bad for our society. In that situation, people always realize that the driver, not the car, is to blame for the crime.

The same goes for stabbings. When we hear about a person being stabbed to death with a knife, our instinct is to blame the criminal who committed the crime, not the knife. I hear about stabbings on the news all the time, and yet I've never seen a rally to ban knives in our country. It's well-understood that knives are not usually used to commit crimes, and it would be illogical to ban them because they do more good than harm. We place the blame on the criminal, not their weapon. For some reason, some people refuse to apply this logic to guns.

Guns, however, just like cars, knives, baseball bats and other potential murder weapons, are much more commonly used for good purposes than for bad ones.

In a given year, guns are used as many as 2.5 million times for self-defense. **This means that each year, firearms are used more than 80 times more often to protect the lives of honest citizens than to take lives**.

Of the 2.5 million times citizens use their guns to defend themselves every year, the overwhelming majority merely brandish their gun or fire a warning shot to scare off their attackers. Less than 8% of the time, a citizen will kill or wound his or her attacker. More often than not, guns are used for good purposes – not bad ones.

I will not argue that guns can never be a tool of murder. Guns along with cars, buses, knives, hammers, shovels, baseball bats, bricks and plastic bags are all things that could be used to take a life. The list goes on and on. Despite the fact that all of these things *could* be used to murder someone, no one argues that all of those items should be banned.

Let's think back to the car example that I talked about earlier. When a crazy person drives a car into a crowd of people, we don't see citizens calling for a nationwide ban on cars. This is because we don't blame the car for the crime. We blame the criminal who drove the car into the crowd of people. Similarly, despite the FBI finding that over 1,500 people in the U.S. were stabbed to death in 2015 (three times more than were killed by shotguns and rifles combined) we don't see a movement to ban knives. We blame the criminal, not the knife. The same logic needs to apply to guns.

In every type of homicide except for homicides committed with a firearm, we blame the criminal, not the weapon. We need to be intellectually consistent. Guns don't commit murders. Criminals commit murders. It is intellectually dishonest to suggest otherwise.

To reduce the number of murders in our country, we need to focus on addressing the root of the problem – the mental health and the education levels of the people who commit the murders. A mentally stable, well-educated person is much less likely to commit a violent crime. A weapon doesn't make someone commit a crime and banning a single type of weapon won't take away a criminal's desire to commit a crime. Murdering someone is already illegal, yet murderers continue to do it. A gun law won't stop them.

Key Points:
- The list of possible murder weapons is never-ending. No one suggests that we ban things like cars, knives, baseball bats, hammers, and plastic bags. We shouldn't treat guns any differently.
- Guns are much more commonly used to save lives than to take them.
- Guns don't commit murders. Criminals commit murders.

We have too many guns in America.

A 2012 study told us that for the first time in American history, we're living in a country with more guns than people. According to the Congressional Research Service, there are well over 300 million firearms in the United States. Gun ownership is at an all-time high.

Are there a lot of guns? Yes. Is this a problem and are there too many? Absolutely not.

The number of guns is increasing over time, yet the violent crime rate has been in decline since the colonial era. According to a study released by the FBI, gun related homicides and crime are "strikingly" down from 20 years ago. A new study by the Pew Research Center shows that U.S. gun homicides rose in the 1960s, gained in the 1970s, peaked in the 1980s and the early 1990s and then plunged and leveled out the past 20 years.

The researchers say, "Despite national attention to the issue of firearm violence most Americans are unaware that gun crime is lower today than it was two decades ago."

More guns are not making us less safe. In fact, it's quite the opposite. The presence of firearms is having a positive impact.

Let's look at an example that most people remember – the shooting at Eugene Simpson Stadium Park in Alexandria, Virginia.

On June 14, 2017, several Republican lawmakers were practicing for the annual Congressional Baseball Game for Charity, scheduled for the following day. While the Congressmen were practicing, a gunman by the name of

James Hodgkinson asked Representatives Ron DeSantis and Jimmy Duncan if it was Republicans or Democrats practicing on the field. Representative Duncan reportedly told the man that it was the Republican team, and minutes later shots were fired. House Majority Whip Steve Scalise of Louisiana was badly injured.

Due to his leadership position, Congressman Steve Scalise had full-time security detail assigned to protect him. After a ten-minute shootout between the gunman and the Capitol and Alexandria police, the shooter was down. As Senator Rand Paul so aptly described, had good guys with guns not been there, "it would've been a massacre."

I do not like to think about what could've happened on that baseball field that day. One reality is that guns saved lives. Another reality is that we cannot always predict when, where, or how a criminal will commit a crime. The best we can do is be ready – anywhere and everywhere – to defend ourselves, our families, and our communities.

Key Points:
- We have more guns than ever in America, yet the violent crime rate in our country has been decreasing since the colonial era.
- We can't anticipate when and where every crime will be committed. Having the ability to defend ourselves in as many places as possible is a very good thing.

The police and government can protect you in times of trouble.

Self-defense is the most fundamental aspect of freedom. It means that you have the ability to defend yourself, your family, and your life from harm. If you must depend on someone else to defend you, by definition you are not free – you're dependent.

Some gun control advocates say that there is no need for private citizens to have weapons because the police and the government can protect you in times of trouble. You don't have to look very far to realize that this isn't true. To address the myth, I've broken it down into two parts: the police protecting you, and the government in general protecting you.

First, let's examine the myth that the police can always protect you in times of trouble. Below I will offer a few examples of times that the police weren't able to protect the lives of innocent civilians in danger.

The Story of Kristi McMains

In January of 2016, a young attorney by the name of Kristi McMains was walking to her car after work. As she headed towards the elevator in the parking garage, she had a sense that something wasn't right. As she got out of the elevator, she ran straight towards her car and before she had a chance to shut the car door she was tackled by her attacker who was armed with a knife.

Kristi reported, "This man quickly overpowered me, stabbed at me with a knife, clamped his hand over my mouth multiple times, and repeatedly tried forcing me into the passenger seat of my car while telling me, "We're going." The entire time this was happening, a rusted, serrated knife was being stabbed towards my abdomen and held at my face. I had been hit in the face, thrown over my driver's side console, and had rips in my tights from his hands trying to force my legs up and over into the passenger seat."

Needless to say, Kristi didn't have a chance to call the police. She did everything she could to defend herself, and used her firearm as a last resort.

Kristi told *FOX News*, "I fought like hell for my life before reaching for my gun. I kicked, I screamed, I had all ten fingernails ripped off and bloodied from scratching and trying to fight my way out of a literal life and death situation. Ultimately, I accessed my gun, shot my attacker multiple times, and saved my life. He will be spending years in prison for what he did to me.[20]"

Kristi didn't have time to wait on the police. *She didn't even have a chance to call them.* It was her against her attacker. No one was there to help. The bottom line is that having a gun saved her life.

The Newark Riots

In 1967, the Newark riot lasted nearly a full week and destroyed millions of dollars of property and real estate. 26 people were killed. Clearly, the police were unable to protect the businesses and their properties, and most importantly the victims.

---

[20] http://www.foxnews.com/opinion/2016/06/02/what-want-to-know-on-gun-violence-awareness-day.html

The Rodney King Riots

In 1992, 53 people were killed in the Rodney King riots, over 2,000 were injured, and in the immediate area over one billion dollars in damages were incurred.

I am not arguing that the police are not a force for good in many instances. Of course, police officers have saved countless innocent lives and there are not enough pages in the world to cite all of those examples. My point is that police officers alone cannot always protect you.

There have been and always will be times when police officers cannot get there in time. If someone breaks into your home with a gun, you can and should call a police officer, but if you're unarmed the reality is that you really can't defend yourself until the cop shows up. If a young lady is walking to her car late at night and someone decides to attack her, she might not have the time to wait for the police. A gun could make the difference between living and dying. In those situations, self-defense is critical. Guns don't guarantee that victims will defeat their attackers, but it sure makes the odds a lot better.

According to the U.S. Department of Justice's Bureau of Justice Statistics, an estimated 3.7 million burglaries occurred each year on average from 2003 to 2007. A household member was present in roughly 1 million burglaries and became victims of violent crimes in 266,560 burglaries]. Again, the police were not able to get there in time. This isn't a shortcoming or an attack on the police, but rather a common-sense conclusion that the police cannot be everywhere at all times.

Now, let's take examine the myth that the government (beyond the police) can protect us in times of trouble.

In order to properly address this myth, we must first reflect on why we have the Second Amendment in the first place. The Second Amendment does not exist merely for us to defend ourselves against a home invasion. The chief purpose of the Second Amendment is to give us, the citizens, the ability to defend ourselves against an oppressive government and those trying to harm us.

Our Founding Fathers knew that the American Revolution could not have happened if the people didn't have the power to resist the state. An armed insurrection was only possible because the power of the arms of the state was equal to the power of the arms of the people. The Founding Fathers understood that governments have oppressed before and could oppress in the future, and they were right.

Adolf Hitler once said, "To conquer a nation, first disarm its citizens." History shows us that Hitler wasn't the only person to follow this logic.

In 1929, Joseph Stalin disarmed his citizens then murdered 20 million of them.

In 1935, Mao Zedong disarmed his citizens then murdered 20 million of them.

In 1938, Adolf Hitler disarmed his citizens then murdered 13 million of them.

In 1956, Pol Pot disarmed his citizens then murdered 2 million of them.

The most oppressive governments in the history of the world became deadly when the people didn't have the ability to defend themselves. Our Founding Fathers wanted to ensure that Americans would always have the ability to resist tyranny should it arise.

Some people argue that due to the advanced military technology that exists today, including tanks and fighter jets, it would be impossible for the people to resist their government, and therefore we shouldn't even try. This argument gives me a lot of pause.

First, if a government is tyrannical and coming after its own citizens, the people should never sit back and let it happen. We teach our children to fight back if they're ever being attacked; why wouldn't we do the same? Secondly, it's wildly inaccurate to assume that the citizens of the United States could not resist a tyrannical military. If we assume that every single person in the military is a trained and qualified infantryman (which they're not), and we account for all 1,281,900 active duty and 811,000 reserve personnel[21], there would 2,092,900 military personnel against us. That's assuming that everyone in the military sides with the government. The United States has an estimated population of 323 million people. It isn't correct to assume that the people wouldn't have the power to fight back.

If we have the Second Amendment to protect us from tyrannical government, how can we count on that very same government to protect us? Certainly, these murderous dictators knew that they couldn't take over without first disarming their citizens. While we surely hope that something as evil as these examples would never happen again, we cannot count on that. We must preserve our right to defend ourselves and ensure that something as evil as this never happens again.

If 'We The People' are going to remain in charge of our government, we cannot give up our right to protect ourselves

---

[21] https://www.defense.gov/News/News-Releases/News-Release-View/Article/652687/department-of-defense-dod-releases-fiscal-year-2017-presidents-budget-proposal/

from our government. Liberty depends upon the Second Amendment and giving that right away is about so much more than just guns. It's about freedom – the freedom to live your life and the freedom to protect yourself against people who try to harm you. No one who believes in freedom should be willing to give that up.

Key Points:
- The police cannot be everywhere at all times. If they were, most of the rapes, burglaries, and murders that happen today would've been prevented by the police before they happened.
- There are plenty of examples of times when the police just didn't get there in time to save an innocent person's life. There are also plenty of examples of times when victims didn't even have the chance to call 911. All of our citizens deserve the right to defend themselves when they're being attacked.
- A key reason why we have the Second Amendment is to defend ourselves from our government should it ever become tyrannical. For this reason alone, it's critical that "We The People" have the right to bear arms. We can't rely on our government to protect us if they're the ones we're fighting against.

5 Common Myths About Hunting And Conservation

I believe that most of the fears and concerns people have about hunting are due to misinformation or a lack of information in general. It is no secret that the anti-hunting community is very vocal and attempts to influence public opinion by advancing untrue statements about hunting and its impact on our word.

If you add up the populations of New York City and Los Angeles, America's two largest cities that population still doesn't surpass the number of people who hunt in America. Despite hunting being so popular and prevalent, there are still a lot of misconceptions about the people who hunt and how they do it. My hope is to correct these fallacies in the next few chapters.

Some people have also been misled to believe that hunting is harmful to animals, the environment, and society is general. The reality is that hunting and conservation go hand in hand. Hunters have an overwhelming positive impact on our world and contribute more to conservation efforts than any other group of people. Hunting also happens to be one of the safest recreational activities that one can participate in, even though the media tries to portray it as the opposite.

If you're going to hold an opinion about hunting, you need to know the facts about the sport. You also must be able to refute the false arguments advanced by its opponents. In the next few chapters I will address the most common myths I hear about hunting and conservation, and provide you with the facts, examples, and logical arguments to support the truth.

Hunting is uniquely dangerous.

A common myth about hunting is that it is uniquely dangerous. This statement couldn't be further from the truth.

In fact, the reality is that the average American does dozens of things every single day that are far more dangerous than hunting. To refute this myth, I'm going to turn to the most recent statistics on hunting-related deaths and accidental deaths in general.

In order to evaluate whether or not hunting is uniquely dangerous, we must first know how many people are injured and killed from hunting each year. According to the International Hunter Education Association, approximately 1,000 people in the U.S. and Canada are accidentally shot by hunters every year, and under 100 of those accidents are fatalities[22]. Most of the victims are hunters, but some non-hunters are injured and killed as well. The per capita rate of accidental gun deaths (including more than just hunting) is approximately 0.18 deaths per 100,000 population[23].

To offer some perspective, I've compiled a list of 10 activities that are far more dangerous than hunting.

Playing Volleyball: Compared to hunting, a person is 11 times more likely to be injured playing volleyball.[24]

---

[22] http://www.ihea-usa.org/_assets/documents/ihea1994.pdf
[23] National Safety Council, Injury Facts 2000 Edition, page 40, and CDC, WISQARS data query website.
[24] https://www.nssf.org/hunting-is-safer-than-golf-and-most-other-recreational-activities/

Snowboarding: Compared to snowboarding, a person is 19 times more likely to be injured snowboarding.[25]

Cheerleading: Compared to hunting, a person is 25 times more likely to be injured cheerleading.[26]

Playing Tackle Football: Compared to hunting, a person is 105 times more likely to be injured cheerleading.[27]

Skateboarding: Compared to hunting, a person is 34 times more likely to be injured while skateboarding.[28]

Playing Soccer: Compared to hunting, a person is 34 times more likely to be injured while playing soccer.[29]

Bicycling: Compared to hunting, a person is 25 times more likely to be injured while riding a bicycle.[30]

---

[25] https://www.nssf.org/hunting-is-safer-than-golf-and-most-other-recreational-activities/

[26] https://www.nssf.org/hunting-is-safer-than-golf-and-most-other-recreational-activities/

[27] https://www.nssf.org/hunting-is-safer-than-golf-and-most-other-recreational-activities/

[28] https://www.nssf.org/hunting-is-safer-than-golf-and-most-other-recreational-activities/

[29] https://www.nssf.org/hunting-is-safer-than-golf-and-most-other-recreational-activities/

[30] https://www.nssf.org/hunting-is-safer-than-golf-and-most-other-recreational-activities/

Tennis: Compared to hunting, a person is nearly 4 times more likely to be injured while playing tennis.[31]

Fishing: Compared to hunting, a person is 4 times more likely to be injured while fishing.[32]

Swimming: The National Safety Council estimates that more than 1,500 die each year in swimming related accidents[33]. This is far more than the number of annual deaths caused by hunting accidents.

In fact, out of 30 activities analyzed in a study conducted by the National Shooting Sports Foundation, hunting with firearms was proven to be the third safest activity, only behind camping and billiards/pool. Activities including bowling, running/jogging, archery, golf, and mountain biking were all found to be more dangerous.[34]

Another study conducted by the National Safety Council tells us that an American's chances of dying are as follows:

In any accident: 1 in 23
By a vehicle while walking: 1 in 612
Fall from bed, chair, furniture: 1 in 4745
Firearm accident: 1 in 4888[35]

---

[31] https://www.nssf.org/hunting-is-safer-than-golf-and-most-other-recreational-activities/
[32] https://www.nssf.org/hunting-is-safer-than-golf-and-most-other-recreational-activities/
[33] http://www.dnr.state.mn.us/hunting/tips/myths.html
[34] http://www.theoutdoorwire.com/media/Hunting-Safe-Activity-Chart-NSSF-branded.jpg
[35] http://www.interstatesportsman.com/articles/how-dangerous-is-hunting-really

According to this study, you are more likely to die from falling than you are from a hunting accident. Looking at these statistics, it's hard to argue that hunting is uniquely dangerous.

In 2014, the most recent year with available data, we see that firearm accidents were among the least common causes of accidental death.

Out of 138,593 accidental deaths in the U.S., 28% were caused by drug poisoning, 24% were caused by motor vehicle traffic accidents (excluding pedal cyclists), 23% were caused by falls, 5% were caused by suffocation, 2.5% were caused by drowning, 2.4% were caused by non-drug poisoning, 1.9% were caused by fire/flame, 1.6% were caused by medical mistakes, 1.2% were caused by natural/environmental factors, 0.7% involved pedal cycles, 0.4% involved guns, and 10% were due to other factors. As you can clearly see, hunting accidents are not a common cause of accidental death.

Guns are involved in 0.4% of accidental deaths among the total population and 1.3% among children. Today, the odds of a child in the U.S. dying in a gun accident are more than a million to one.[36]

---

[36] https://www.nraila.org/issues/gun-safety/

It's also important to note that throughout the past 20 years, the annual number of gun-related accidental deaths has decreased by more than half[37]. At the same time, American gun ownership has reached an all-time high.[38]

Hunting accidents are also in decline. This is believed to be due to an increase in education and better safety practices, two measures that all hunters support.

Every statistic proves to us that hunting is anything but uniquely dangerous. Unfortunately, many people in the anti-gun community use fear tactics and false information to advance a different narrative. When you dig into the facts and look at the research, it becomes clear that hunting is one of the safest activities in which a person can participate.

---

[37] https://www.fbi.gov/news/stories/latest-crime-statistics-released
[38] http://money.cnn.com/2016/08/24/news/chicago-gun-control/index.html

Hunters are bloodthirsty, inconsiderate people who don't care for animals or nature.

People who oppose hunting frequently attack the character of those who hunt. I believe this is due in part to an awful stereotype that has been established and advanced through our culture.

Hunters are not what they're sometimes portrayed to be. They don't wake up, grab a gun, and shoot anything that moves. They don't kill animals for fun and leave them in the fields to die a long, painful death. That just isn't reality.

The truth is that hunters are some of the most resourceful, considerate, respectful, generous, hardworking, and mindful people that I know. Their motivation to hunt is not to destroy wildlife, but rather to spend time exploring and appreciating the world that we live in. The left will try their hardest to make you think otherwise.

This quote is the first thing you see on PETA's hunting page:

> *Hunting might have been necessary for human survival in prehistoric times, but today most hunters stalk and kill animals merely for the thrill of it, not out of necessity. This unnecessary, violent form of "entertainment" rips animal families apart and leaves*

countless animals orphaned or badly injured when hunters miss their targets.[39]

This argument is false on every front. I explain the necessity of hunting in a future chapter, but for now I'll address the point about killing animals for the thrill of it.

I've spent time with dozens of avid hunters, and not a single one has told me that they hunt for the thrill of it. Of course, my experience isn't a scientific study, so I'll turn to one. There are hundreds of reasons to hunt, but according to a 2013 study, the most common reason people hunt is to gather their own food.[40] Other common reasons include spending time with friends and family and spending time in nature. A hunter's motivation is not to destroy our ecosystems or to harm as many animals as possible. Their goal is to provide for themselves while experiencing all that our world has to offer.

Another important reality to consider is that most wild animals don't pass away naturally in comfort. They definitely don't die a quick and sedated death with the help of veterinary medicine. Pheasants, for example, are usually caught by a hawk or a fox then eaten alive. This causes a long and unbearably painful death for the bird. Most wildlife experts will agree that being eaten alive is one of the most horrible ways for an animal to die. Hunting offers a much faster and painless death.

---

[39] https://www.peta.org/issues/animals-in-entertainment/cruel-sports/hunting/

[40] http://www.fieldandstream.com/blogs/wild-chef/2013/10/study-shows-more-hunters-are-it-meat

A friend once told me that the most horrible thing he ever witnessed was watching a zebra be eaten alive by a pack of lions in Africa. The lions literally chomped away, piece by piece, at the dying zebra. It seems to me that nature has a much more cruel and bloodthirsty approach. A bullet through the heart seems like a much more peaceful way to die. If animal rights activists truly care about eliminating violent animal deaths, they should focus on deaths caused by other animals, not people.

Natural predatory death for animals is much more painful than death by a bow or bullet. Hunters do intensive research and study of exactly how to kill an animal to ensure the least amount of pain possible. Hunters do not find pleasure in seeing animals suffer, unlike what most anti-hunting advocates will try to tell you. People who hunt do everything humanly possible to make kills quick, safe and as respectable to nature and the wildlife as possible.

Left-wing activists with an anti-gun agenda and groups like PETA try to defame hunters and label them as things they're not. This is a tactic used by the left to brand hunters as bad people and turn the mainstream culture against them.

Let's look at a specific example of this practice:

"I believe that hunting desensitizes the hunter to pain, suffering and death, and that this lessening of what may be a natural compassion for other living creatures is not limited to non-human animals. I further believe that this inability to empathize is not healthy for members of a society trying to live together in peace and indeed, is not healthy for a society and its relations with other political entities in the world."

Dr. Priscilla Cohn, The Committee to Abolish Sport Hunting

This statement, which is more of an assumption and opinion than anything else, is incredibly misleading and downright false. To disprove Dr. Cohn's bold claim, I will first discuss how hunters truly view hunting and killing and then review some actual scientific data that proves her claim to be incorrect.

Dr. Cohn presents the argument that hunters lose compassion for animals after years of hunting. She even goes as far as to say that this desensitization bleeds over into human relations.

Most hunters I know and have had the pleasure of meeting are some of the most mild mannered, responsible business owners in the country. Almost all of them have a common thread that ties them together -- a deep care and love for wildlife and their families. Almost all hunters own dogs and treat them like their own children. Contrary to what Dr. Cohn argues, hunters do not abuse animals they come in contact with, but rather the opposite is true. They develop a deeper appreciation for wildlife through their hunting experiences. They learn more about the unique qualities of wildlife and consider hunting an animal to be a testament to its beauty and greatness. For example, some of the top hunters in the world have trophies of big game they have shot in Africa. When you ask them about the animal they don't say, "Oh, that stupid thing on the wall, I can't wait to shoot another one of those things." Instead they say something along the lines of, "That lion on the wall is one of the most beautiful things I have ever seen. The way it graced the wetlands and brush ever so gracefully, the way it arose from a nap under a giant tree in the afternoon. I was proud to have been able to interact with such a beautiful creature."

One of my great friends happens to be an award-winning hunter and one of the top hunters in the history of the sport. He once told me, "I can't even tell you how many hunts I have been on where I never pulled the trigger. Sometimes I did not run across something I felt comfortable killing, other times the wildlife was just too beautiful. It is not about the killing. It is about being outside and enjoying the wildlife." He doesn't hunt to harm animals, but rather to learn about the world we live in while enjoying and learning about wildlife.

Another seasoned hunter who has spent months at a time hunting in Africa tells a story of one of his favorite hunting trips.

"I arose early one day right at daybreak and in the distance under a tree I saw a mother leopard playing with her new born babies. I made my way over behind a bush where she could not see me. Seeing her play with her cubs under the tree it seemed as if they were almost smiling at each other. Every night I went over to that tree and I left a little piece of meat for the baby leopards to climb up and eat.

I woke up earlier each morning to go over there and see what the baby leopard would do that morning. I got so much joy from seeing the leopards grow up in front of my eyes as they showed great perseverance to continually go up the tree with all their willpower just to get the piece of meat I left for them. I knew I was in great risk for if the mother knew I was just 20 feet away, I may have been a dead man. It never even

crossed my mind to shoot either the mom or the cubs.
Some things are just too beautiful to kill."

Both of those stories are from some of the most experienced hunters on the planet. They have killed many different kind of game all across the world, yet contrary to Dr. Cohn's claim, they don't develop a pleasure for killing or lose a sense of beauty and appreciation around them. They respect, appreciate, and honor nature.

Another part of Dr. Cohn's statement alleges that hunting has a negative impact on human relationships.

Luckily there have been many studies on this topic that have directly studied the relationship between violence and hunting. Perhaps the most relevant to this myth was a study done by Chris Eskridge, a criminologist from Nebraska.

At the end of his study Eskridge concluded that as hunting licenses sales go up, violent crime rates go down. He even factored population density and income levels into the study to account for that possible impact. Eskridge argued that hunting serves as a constructive outlet for many types of stress and tensions that otherwise could contribute to violent behavior.

There is an abundance of additional research to support this idea. The research shows that when people enjoy more sport shooting, it may contribute to inner-peace and increased social stability.

Another world-renowned criminologist from Florida State, Gary Kleck, concluded after years of research that "gun owners are not, as a group, psychologically abnormal, nor are they more racist, sexist, or pro-violent than non-owners are."

Other studies have shown that almost 70 percent of hunters are motivated to hunt each year because they have a psychological connection with nature that they feel is exclusive to hunting. Some even said they believe hunting helps improve their mental health. Dr. Cohn's claim that hunting has a negative impact on human relationships is simply false. There is no evidence to back-up that claim, but there is ample evidence to refute it.

Generally speaking, hunters are law-abiding citizens. They pay for hunting licenses and permits, follow the hunting regulations set forth by local and state government, and support conservation with their money and their time. The actions of hunters prove that they care deeply about animals and their environment. They clean-up what they kill. They use every part of the animal possible. They don't kill more than they can eat.

Hunters are also extremely committed to practicing safe techniques and following proper safety procedures at all times. Almost every state in the US requires that hunters pass a course to get a hunting license. Because of their high-regard for education and safety, hunters are a lot less likely to cause or be involved in a gun accident compared to a non-hunter. As I discussed at length in the previous chapter, hunting is one the safest sports in which a person can participate, further proving that hunters are not creating danger for our society.

A recent study conducted by Lizotte and Sheppard analyzed a group of high school students from Rochester, New York and found that students who were taught to use a gun and owned a gun with legal parent supervision had lower rates of crime, drug use and delinquency than their peers who had never come across guns before in their life. Given this discovery, it's hard to argue that hunters and responsible gun owners are making society less safe.

It is important to remember that hunters are normal people, and hunting is more common that some people think. You might be surprised to know that celebrities including Madonna, Peyton Manning, Avril Lavigne, Eva Longoria-Parker, Shaquille O'Neal, Kurt Russell, and Jennifer Lawrence are all dedicated hunters. U.S. President and avid sportsman-hunter Theodore Roosevelt created our first national parks and forever protected over 230 million acres for wildlife and public use.[41] In fact, a majority of all U.S. Presidents have been hunters. Hunters are not evil, bloodthirsty people; they're respectable men, women, and young people from all walks of life.

---

[41]http://www.rmef.org/Conservation/HuntingIsConservation/25 ReasonsWhyHuntingIsConservation.aspx

Hunting harms animal migration.

A common argument made by anti-hunting activists is that hunting harms animal migration and livelihood. PETA's website claims, "Hunting disrupts migration and hibernation patterns and destroys families."[42]

Unfortunately, PETA's website does not go into detail or defend their claim that hunting disrupts migration, nor do they defend their claim that hunting disrupts hibernation patterns. By issuing this statement PETA demonizes the entire hunting community by suggesting that hunters have directly contributed to migratory patterns being skewed and thrown off and hibernation cycles being disrupted.

Perhaps the best way to refute this myth is to share the story of Ducks Unlimited and how hunters singlehandedly saved the waterfowl population in the United States.

It was 1937, and just seven years after the Great Depression. The devastating and disastrous Dust Bowl had dried up thousands of feeding areas for ducks all across the Midwest, and there was an evident decrease in the presence of ducks. Not wishing to exacerbate the problem, hunters hesitated to hunt or shoot any ducks at all during this period of time. Many feared that this natural disaster would be the permanent end to waterfowl as they knew it.

One hunter recalled during this period of time, "It wasn't worth getting up early anymore to go hunt. Why should I go to my favorite spots just to see empty skies?" This time period quickly became known as the "Duck Depression."

---

[42] https://www.peta.org/issues/wildlife/wildlife-factsheets/sport-hunting-cruel-unnecessary/

The solution was bold. A small but mighty group of seasoned hunters from across the country got together and formulated a substantive plan to rejuvenate the waterfowl population in North America. Their plan would transcend the U.S./Canadian border in an attempt to bring back the waterfowl population to its earlier prominence. They did not turn to the government or an animal protection agency, but instead they stepped up and did it themselves. Together these hunters formulated a plan to multiply the population over an entire continent.

Trying to understand why the population was in such a steep decline, they organized massive surveys all across Canada and the United States. It laid a baseline for the current population and gave them additional information about waterfowl migration.

After carefully analyzing their research, the hunters determined that they needed to invest time and money into what was known as the "Duck Factory" or the Canadian wetlands. This is where a majority of the waterfowl went to feed and live during the year before migration season.

During the first year, Ducks Unlimited planned to cultivate over one hundred thousand acres for conservation. They targeted three specific wetlands that they would work on in an attempt to bring back waterfowl breeding to those areas.

They worked with local farmers to create more efficient irrigation techniques that would not drain as much water away from the breeding grounds. As Ducks Unlimited began to gain notoriety, the press began to say "This is not just an organization for sport, but this is a group of people committed to truly saving a specific specie and making sure they are going to be there for the next generation. Their commitment to saving the migratory patterns of waterfall and fostering them for their kids and grandkids has been unparalleled to this time."

After one year of work and just eight months in the field, Ducks Unlimited cultivated over 110,000 acres of feeding and breeding grounds for waterfowl. All of this commitment and time had resulted in vast multiplication of ducks and geese in the years that followed.

Ducks Unlimited expanded and took on many more projects all across North America, focusing specifically on conservation. Through the 1950s and 1960s, a huge wave of grassroots support came in for Ducks Unlimited. Hunters all across North America pitched in money, time, and land, and helped in any way possible to further the conservation projects in which Ducks Unlimited was involved.

In the early 1980's it became evident a strategy was needed for waterfowl that were stopping on their migratory patterns all through North America. Studies were done to analyze migratory patterns and began restoring lakes and reservoirs in regions where waterfowl usually stop on their way south. Ducks Unlimited began opening offices in different parts of the country, so they could offer unique regionalized conservation techniques for ducks and geese that were migrating south or returning north.

Over 75 years of work and commitment, Ducks Unlimited has influenced over 95 million acres for the benefit of waterfowl in North America. Rough figures show that Ducks Unlimited played an instrumental role in preserving and fostering close to 1 billion waterfowl. For these reasons is why over half a million members every year give money, time, and energy to make sure waterfowl will be there for the next generation.

Hunting was the reason these initiatives were started. True conservationists are indeed hunters. It began with a handful of dedicated outdoorsmen who loved to shoot, and who refused to accept that fact that autumn skies would not be filed with duck and geese. They refused to accept that waterfowl would no longer be able to be hunted and enjoyed on a widespread scale.

Hunting does not "throw off migratory patterns" as PETA claimed, in fact hunting and hunters have saved migratory patterns, and actually improved them. Due to the investments they have made in wetlands and marshes there are more ducks and geese in North America than at any other time in history.

Hunting is no longer needed in modern society.

For thousands of years, human beings hunted the food they ate in order to survive. In many cases, people got their food, clothing, shelter, and tools all from the animals they killed. In those times hunting was definitely a necessity because hunting meant eating. The ability to hunt literally made the difference between life or death.

Today, most Americans get their food from grocery stores, and they don't need to personally go out and hunt to provide themselves with basic necessities like clothing, shelter, and tools. For most Americans, hunting on a regular basis is not necessary for survival, but it is an activity that millions of people still enjoy each year.

Because hunting isn't a necessary activity for every American in the United States, some people believe that hunting is longer needed in our society and therefore the practice should cease to exist. I fundamentally disagree with this argument for several reasons.

First, if we decided to ban everything that is not necessary for survival the minute someone does not like it, we would live in a very boring, do-nothing society in which people exist merely to breathe, sleep, and eat fruits and vegetables (although, I am sure in today's world you would find people who take offense to those activities, too!). You do not have to love hunting or participate in the sport, but you should respect other people's freedom to participate in activities they enjoy that don't cause harm to you. There are plenty of things in our society that we don't need -- lavish cars, big homes, and

Netflix to name a few. Does the fact that we could live without them mean that we shouldn't have them? Of course not. Necessity is not the standard for deciding what is permitted in society. The same logic must apply to hunting.

It is essential to note that for many people in America hunting is still a very necessary aspect of their livelihood. Today, the hunting industry sustains more than 680,000 jobs in America.[43] Eliminating the hunting industry would have a devastating impact on our economy, and directly impact hundreds of thousands of hunters as well as non-hunters and their families. In addition to the jobs provided by the hunting industry, it is estimated that the hunting community pumps over $24.9 billion dollars into the economy each year.[44] This money goes to much more than just guns and ammunition. Hunters spend an estimated $2.1 billion per year on food and drinks during hunting trips.[45] They also spend millions on fuel, trailers, hotels, motels, clothing, hunting gear, and accessories, all of which pump money into our economy and sustain thousands of jobs for Americans across the country. Hunters spend more on their activities than the total annual revenue of the McDonald's Corporation.[46] Looking more globally, the research firm Southwick Associates found that hunters pump more than $426 million into the African economy each year and support 53 million jobs on that

---

[43]http://www.rmef.org/Conservation/HuntingIsConservation/25Rea sonsWhyHuntingIsConservation.aspx

[44]http://sportsmenslink.org/uploads/page/Bright%20Stars%20of%2 0the%20Economy.pdf?phpMyAdmin=718c504f43d4t2bb2bf15

[45]http://sportsmenslink.org/uploads/page/Bright%20Stars%20of%2 0the%20Economy.pdf?phpMyAdmin=718c504f43d4t2bb2bf15

[46]http://sportsmenslink.org/uploads/page/Bright%20Stars%20of%2 0the%20Economy.pdf?phpMyAdmin=718c504f43d4t2bb2bf15

continent.[47] Hunting is a critical part of sustaining societies all across the world. You might not think hunting is necessary, but the people who depend on the hunting industry for survival will surely disagree.

To some people, hunting is also their way of accessing organic, free-range meat for their family. The animal meat that comes from hunting does not go through the same chemical processes as grocery store meat, and therefore is viewed by some as a more organic and healthy option. To people who value access to untreated, free-range meat that they hunt themselves, hunting is definitely an important part of their livelihood.

It is also important to recognize that hunting is absolutely necessary if you wish to consume animal products in general. Most of the beef that Americans consume comes from cows that are raised in farms and then led to slaughterhouses in which the cattle enter as live animals and leave as fresh cuts of meat. If you know anything about how the majority of chickens are raised and killed in slaughterhouses, you must certainly agree that being hunted in the wild is a better way to die. Hunting is a more humane method of obtaining animal meat for consumption. A 2013 study found that the most common reason hunters went into the fields was "for the meat."[48] It is not intellectually honest to argue that hunting is not necessary but eating animal products is acceptable and permitted.

---

[47] http://www.petersenshunting.com/conservation-politics/6-examples-where-hunting-helped-preserve-wildlife/
[48] http://www.fieldandstream.com/blogs/wild-chef/2013/10/study-shows-more-hunters-are-it-meat

Lastly, if you fall into the category of people who value conservation efforts and wish to preserve natural resources, hunting is absolutely necessary. Every single day U.S. sportsmen contribute $8 million to conservation. Through state licenses and fees, hunters contribute over $796 million per year for conservation programs in the United States. An 11% tax on guns, ammo, bows and arrows generates $371 million a year for conservation.[49]

Hunters are also responsible for conserving and restoring important natural resources and saving populations of numerous species over the years including ducks, turkeys, whitetails.[50] The hunting community does considerably more for conservation than the government or any other group of people, and if you value conservation, you need to thank American hunters.

Hunting is absolutely necessary in today's society. Without it, hundreds of thousands of Americans would lose their jobs, conservation funds would be depleted, and efforts to protect and conserve our environment would reach an all-time low. While every American family may not need to hunt their own food and depend on animals for clothing, shelter, and household tools, hunting has an overwhelmingly positive impact for both the hunting and non-hunting communities.

---

[49]http://www.rmef.org/Conservation/HuntingIsConservation/25 ReasonsWhyHuntingIsConservation.aspx

[50]http://www.rmef.org/Conservation/HuntingIsConservation/25 ReasonsWhyHuntingIsConservation.aspx

Hunting is cruel to animals and the environment they live in.

Some people believe that hunting is cruel to animals and harmful to their environments. Out of all the myths I've addressed so far, this one might be the most ridiculous claim.

First, let's talk about the financial impact that hunters have on animals and their environments. In 1937, the hunting community *requested* an 11% tax on guns, ammo, bows and arrows to help fund conservation efforts across the United States. Every year, hunters pay more than $1.6 million for conservation programs across America. As of 2013, that tax had raised over $8 billion for conservation. Because of this and other fees, hunters and fisherman together fund nearly 75% of the annual income for conservation agencies in all 50 states.[51] Hunters are anything but harmful to the environment -- they're the environment's biggest financial supporters!

In addition to supporting conservation efforts financially, the hunting community is actively involved in preserving and protecting a wide range of species. In many cases, hunters are to thank for preventing a species from going extinct. The examples below demonstrate the incredibly positive impact that hunters have had on animals, the environment, and society in general.

Hunters help manage growing numbers of predators including cougars, bears, coyotes, and wolves. While government agencies spend millions of

---

[51]http://www.rmef.org/Conservation/HuntingIsConservation/25 ReasonsWhyHuntingIsConservation.aspx

dollars to control predators and varmints, hunters are more than willing to pay for that opportunity.

In 1907, North America had only 41,000 elk. Thanks to the money and hard work invested by hunters to restore and conserve their natural habitat, there are more than 1 million elk in the wild today.[52]

In 1900, North America had only 500,000 whitetails remaining. Thanks to the conservation work spearheaded by hunters, today there are more than 32 million.[53]

In 1900, only 100,000 wild turkeys remained. Thanks to hunters, there are over 7 million in existence today.[54]

In 1950, we had only 12,000 pronghorn. Thanks to hunters, today there are more than 1.1 million.[55]

Hunters historically are the most creative and committed conservationists. They use their time, talent, and treasure to preserve wildlife and game for the next generation. They not only care about conservation, but they're very effective at it.

As you can see, this is just one example of the hunting community having a profoundly positive impact on our environment. When a species was in danger, hunters stepped up to investigate the issue and solve it. This story is

---

[52]http://www.rmef.org/Conservation/HuntingIsConservation/25 ReasonsWhyHuntingIsConservation.aspx

[53] https://www.nrahlf.org/articles/2016/7/22/20-reasons-why-hunting-is-conservation/

[54] https://www.nrahlf.org/articles/2016/7/22/20-reasons-why-hunting-is-conservation/

[55]http://www.rmef.org/Conservation/HuntingIsConservation/25 ReasonsWhyHuntingIsConservation.aspx

a testament to the hunting community's deep commitment to conservation and goes to show that hunters are not the cruel and inconsiderate people that others sometimes make them out to be.

Time and time again, it has been proven that hunters are extremely committed to protecting our environment and all of the animals who inhabit it.

It's not about guns.

It's about control.

To the left, gun control isn't really about guns. It's about control.

> "Unfortunately you've grown up hearing voices that incessantly warn of government as nothing more than some separate, sinister entity that's at the root of all of our problems. Some of these same voices do their best to gum up the works. They'll warn that tyranny is always lurking just around the corner. You should reject these voices. Because what they suggest is that our brave and creative and unique experiment in self rule is somehow just a sham with which we can't be trusted."
> -President Barack Obama

I never thought that President Obama understood our Constitution, but this is an especially concerning statement.

Sadly, I hear this rhetoric repeated on an ongoing basis from professors, friends, and college students who truly believe that governmental tyranny is unrealistic and could never happen in America. These people believe that governments like ours can't go rogue, and that our American system of government is exempt from experiencing civil unrest. Despite their optimism, history proves otherwise.

Nazi Germany and Stalin's dictatorship are just two examples of governments gone bad. If you look closely, you will see that the first step to totalitarian government was unilateral disarmament.

Shortly after World War I, Germany instituted a gun control policy that made it extremely hard to access and purchase a gun. Every gun owner was required to have a permit, which was expensive and hard to come by. When the Nazis took power in 1933, they went home to home conducting searches and demanding firearms from the citizens.

They did not just make it illegal to own certain guns and firearms. They went door to door in an extremely aggressive manner prying guns away from ordinary people all in the name of "public safety."

Shortly after, one of the biggest riots in Nazi history took place. The famous riot was called "Kristallnacht" meaning "the night of broken glass." Nazi forces raided and plundered Jewish business and religious centers.

Just three days after Kristallnacht, Adolf Hitler issued an executive order making it illegal for any Jewish person to own or possess a firearm. This was the beginning of the Holocaust, and by all means the end of Jewish freedom in Germany. As soon as the Jews lost their right to bear arms, they lost every other freedom they enjoyed including the freedom of expression, thought, religion, and even their right to life.

Germany was able to confiscate weapons extremely easily because they spent years registering every single gun with a location and address tied to it. When it came to confiscate the guns from the Jews, the Gestapo had a national database that specified where every single gun was located. It made the confiscation process seamless.

The Soviet Union had a very similar situation. After the Red victory in the Civil War, all firearms were made illegal. If someone was found in possession of a firearm they would be sentenced to hard labor. In 1925, the law was made more severe by adding a fine of 300 rubles to the penalty for firearm ownership.

Stalin eventually went as far as to ban knifes in 1935. He made the penalty up to five years in prison and even sentenced some individuals to death for owning a knife.

Once Stalin was able to institute his policies to disarm the masses, he began his massive campaign to kill millions of his own citizens. In a ten year span, he killed over ten million people. He was able to successfully execute this massive extermination plan because the citizenry was unarmed and unable to resist his tyrannical campaign.

Another example was in 1956 when Cambodia instituted strict gun control policy and disallowed any citizens from owning guns. Shortly after that policy was enacted, the government killed over one million defenseless people in cold blood. The people of Cambodia had no way of protecting themselves against a tyrannical government. They were slaughtered by the hundreds of thousands as the government pushed forth their cleansing campaign.

When a government confiscates guns or advances any kind of restrictive gun control measures, it is not about guns, but rather it is about control. History is filled with countless examples of governments that turn tyrannical. Some people call those who fear tyranny "conspiracy theorists," but I urge those people to take a close look at world history.

The only way to truly protect freedom and liberty in our country is to protect the Second Amendment. People who want to take away that right are focused on control, not guns.

How To Win The Debate

It is no secret that people are very passionate about the Second Amendment debate. There are many strong opinions held on both sides of the issue, and it seems to be a favorite issue to debate. This is a good thing. Debates are a very effective way to spread the truth, refute the lies, and win over hearts and minds to our side.

Debating can be scary, but I believe that with practice, preparation, and a little bit of experience it becomes much easier. Debating is really nothing more than having a discussion.

I have compiled the following tips to help you become a more effective debater, specifically when you're debating a topic that relates to the Second Amendment.

1. **Know who you're trying to convince.**

    An important part of winning any debate is knowing your audience and understanding who you're really trying to convince. Often times, it's not the person you're debating that you're trying to win over. It's your audience.

    People who are neutral or undecided on an issue will rarely engage in a debate. You will usually find these people sitting on the sidelines taking in information that they hear from both sides. They are there to learn. Whether it's students observing a classmate debate their teacher, or a group of people watching a heated debate develop on a Facebook status, nearly every debate has an audience. Know your audience and make your arguments for them. These are the people you are most likely to influence.

When you're debating someone who is very committed to their ideals, it is unlikely that you will convince them to change their position. Whenever you engage in a discussion about a hot button issue, think about your potential to influence your audience and debate with them in mind.

2. Know your facts.

There is no substitute for knowing the facts. Nothing will ever substitute knowledge and it is important to keep our arguments rooted in facts. Read anything and everything and stay up to date with current events and arguments coming from *both* sides of the issue.

If you aren't sure where to start, I recommend finding a few news websites that you like and making it a habit to check them every single day. Spending even 10-15 minutes per day skimming through the news will make you so much more informed. If that doesn't work for you, try watching the news on TV while you get ready in the morning or subscribing to push notifications from news apps on your phone. Whatever you decide to do, make it a habit and stick to it. There are so many ways to access the news that you're bound to find something that works for you. The more you know, the more comfortable you'll feel when you're debating your ideas.

3. Ask questions to make your best points.

One of the most effective ways to make your point in a debate is to ask questions of your opponent. When others are spewing out emotionally charged arguments, the best way to disarm and gain the lead in an argument is to ask questions based in facts. Use the questions as a tool for reshaping the argument to show the wicked truth in theirs. For example, if someone is spewing out propaganda on how gun-free zones would solve our mass shooting problems, all you have to ask is, "Sir or Madam, how is it explained that over 98% of mass shootings in the last 50 years took place in gun free zones?" Make your opponent answer for their arguments. It is easy to ignore a statement in a debate, but it is very hard to ignore a question.

4. **Be honest when don't know something.**

We all have a lot to learn. When you're in a debate you have nothing to gain by making up facts and trying to hide the fact that you don't know something. If your opponent mentions an issue, event, or statistic that you're unfamiliar with, it is a good idea to just admit it. Say something like, "I'm not familiar with that event so I can't comment on it. I will have to look into it." You won't look weak or uneducated; you'll look intellectually honest and most people will respect you for it.

Admitting what you don't know is always better than getting caught it up an argument you can't win. If you know your facts and have great points to make, admitting that you don't know it all won't be a problem.

5. **Be mindful of your tone.**

No one likes a jerk. As human beings we have a tendency to naturally gravitate towards people and ideas that make us feel good. We want to associate ourselves and our thoughts with uplifting, positive things. This is why companies will typically hire cheerful, upbeat individuals for their sales teams. They know that people are less likely to buy from an angry, grumpy jerk.

When you're debating, you're essentially "selling" your ideas to your audience. For the same reasons that salespeople need to be upbeat and cheerful, you need to be positive, kind, and compassionate. Never get angry, raise your voice, or make personal attacks. If your opponent gets personal, be the better person and refuse to go that low.

If you are able to come across as a respectful, kind, and genuinely considerate person, your audience will be much more likely to consider and accept your ideas. Always be mindful of your tone and approach. Style is just as important as substance.

6. **Know when to walk away.**

Sometimes the most important part of winning a debate is knowing when it is time to cut it off and walk away. As I mentioned earlier, you're most likely to change your audience's perspective -- not the perspective of the person you're debating. Because your focus is on the spectators, you need to be mindful of when continuing to debate will hurt your cause rather than help it.

When you've made all of your points, refuted all of your opponent's false claims, and find yourself only talking in circles, it is time to cut it off.

Debating can be intimidating at first, but I truly believe that the more you practice the more comfortable you will feel about it. When you debate in front of an audience, whether that's your peers, your classmates, or your Facebook friends, you're helping undecided, uninformed minds form opinions about important issues. I urge you to always be prepared to defend your ideas. Our movement will only grow if we are successful at persuading people to adopt our point of view.

A Call To Action

There are a lot of people who want to see our Second Amendment go away, and they're more organized, determined, and committed than ever to make that happen.

I have learned a lot throughout my time leading Turning Point USA, but one of the most important things I have realized is that The Left will stop at *nothing* to win. They are organized, trained, equipped, and well-funded. They are misinformed, but they are working hard to advance their ideas. Our side must be up for the challenge.

I hope that you will use the knowledge you gained from this book to help you be an active and articulate voice for freedom and liberty. There are many ways to make a difference -- from being an activist on campus to joining a non-profit organization to helping us achieve political victories.

You can also make a difference by simply talking to your friends. I have found that the most powerful voices for change are often not the politicians or the celebrities, but rather the moms, dads, sisters, brothers, friends, and peers of the uninformed. People are most influenced by others who are close to them. When you share a Second Amendment Facebook post or share your opinion over coffee, you are making a difference. If you are an articulate, kind, and informed voice for your beliefs, you will be surprised by how many people you can influence and win over.

I know that it can be uncomfortable to speak out, especially in today's political climate where differing opinions are not always tolerated. It can be scary to share your opinion. I urge you to do it anyways. Our movement and our

Second Amendment need you, and I promise that it gets easier with practice.

Hunting is important. Guns are important. In some cases, these are life or death issues. When given the opportunity, I hope you will use your voice to spread the truth about hunting, guns, and the Second Amendment.

The Second Amendment is the cornerstone of American freedom and liberty in our country. Without it, all other rights, freedoms, and privileges are lost. There is a very dedicated and organized movement working 24/7 to take away our Second Amendment. They are fighting this battle on every front -- culturally, politically, and in our classrooms -- and it is up to us to do something about it.

You do not need to do everything, but I believe everyone can do something. I hope you will consider finding a way to use your gifts, time, and talent to defend our Second Amendment. There is so much at stake, and the future of liberty and freedom in America depends on us. **We need to spread the truth and correct the lies.**